MW00911355

this gift is for

_____

from

_____

Prayers

A
JANET
THOMA
BOOK

THOMAS NELSON PUBLISHERS
Nashville

CONTENTS

"And when the times come when we can't pray, it is very simple: if Jesus is in my heart let Him pray, let me allow Him to pray in me, to talk to his Father in the silence of my heart. Since I cannot speak— He will pray."

—Mother Theresa

In Times
of Joy

Now as we come to the setting of the sun, and our eyes behold the vesper light, we sing your praises O God: Father, Son, and Holy Spirit.
—Book of Common Prayer

Most high, all-powerful sweet Lord, yours is the praise, the glory, and the honor and every blessing.
—Francis of Assisi

To see a World in a Grain of
  Sand
And a Heaven in a Wildflower,
Hold Infinity in the palm of your
  hand
And Eternity in an hour.

—William Blake

Glory be to God for dappled things.

—Gerard Manley Hopkins

Blessed are you because you have
   made me glad.
It has not turned out as I
   expected.

               —Tobit 8:16a

Open our eyes to behold thy gracious hand in all thy works; that, rejoicing in thy whole creation, we may learn to serve thee with gladness; for the sake of him through whom all things were made.

—Book of Common Prayer

Holy Spirit, giving life to all life, moving all creatures, root of all things, washing them clean, . . . you are our true life, luminous, wonderful, awakening the heart from its ancient sleep.

—Hildegard of Bingen

In Times
of Doubt

Though I am His sheep, I am still
  prone to stray.
So Jesus in love sends afflictions
  my way;
The lessons that come in this
  school of deep pain
Will teach me to follow my Lord
  once again!

—Bosch

16

'Twas He who taught me thus to
    pray
And I know He has answered
    prayer,
But it has been in such a way
As almost drove me to despair.
                    —**Anon.**

Never doubt in the dark what God told you in the light.
—V. Raymond Edman

Life has no question that faith cannot answer.

—Thomas L. Johns

Faith is the final triumph over incongruity, the final assertion of the meaningfulness of existence.

—Reinhold Niebuhr

We are told
to wait on You
but, Lord,
there is no time.
My heart implores
upon its knees
. . . hurry,
please!
—Ruth Bell Graham

I lay my "Whys"
before Your Cross in worship
    kneeling,
my mind too numb for thought,
my heart beyond all feeling.
And worshipping,
realize that I in knowing You
    don't need a "why."
            —Ruth Graham

Dear Lord, my heart is burdened
   down—
I'll leave it all to You;
But as I trust and think and pray,
Please show me what to do.

—**Branon**

Remind me, O Lord,
that faith makes things possible,
not easy.

—Anon.

Holy Wind,
　　Blow across my mind,
Free me
　　Of the things that bind.

—Anon.

Lord, turn my mountain of doubt into a mustard seed of faith.

—Anon.

For
Comfort

"Courage is fear that has said its prayers."

—Karle Wilson Baker

I will abide in Your tabernacle
   forever;
I will trust in the shelter of Your
   wings.

Selah.
—Ps. 61:4

29

"There are no hopeless situations; there are only people who have grown hopeless about them."

—**Marshall Foch**

You will keep him in perfect
   peace,
Whose mind is stayed on You,
Because he trusts in You.
   —Isa. 26:3

But I am poor and needy;
Yet the LORD thinks upon me.
You are my help and my
    deliverer;
Do not delay, O my God.

—Ps. 40:17

Do not leave me nor forsake me,
O God of my salvation.
When my father and mother
　forsake me,
Then the LORD will take care of
　me.

—Ps. 27:9b,10

[Lord] my heart is a lonely hunter
that hunts on a lonely hill.
—**William Sharp**

Turn Yourself to me,
and have mercy on me,
For I am desolate and afflicted.
The troubles of my heart have
    enlarged;
Oh, bring me out of my distress.
—Ps. 25:16,17

The deepest need of man is the need to overcome his separateness, to leave the prison of his aloneness.

—Erich Fromm

The soul hardly ever realizes it, but whether he is a believer or not, his loneliness is really a homesickness for God.

—Hubert van Zeller

Dear God . . .
Be good to me.
The sea is so wide
and my boat is so small.

—Old Fisherman's Prayer

Of
Forgiveness

I loved thee late,
Ah, late I loved thee, Lord,
Yet not so late but how dost still
    afford
The proof that thou wilt bear,
    with winning art,
One sinner more upon thy loving
    heart.

—Augustine

And forgive us our debts,
As we forgive our debtors.

—Matt. 6:12

A wise man will make haste to forgive, because he knows the true
value of time.

—Samuel Johnson

Forgive the many errors that I
   made yesterday
And let me try again, dear God,
To walk closer in thy way.
      —Helen Steiner Rice

Teach me to feel another's woe,
To hide the fault I see;
That mercy I to others show,
That mercy shown to me.

—Pope

Look on my affliction and my
  pain,
And forgive all my sins.

—Ps. 25:18

"Let not this weak, unknowing
   hand
Presume Thy bolts to throw
And deal damnation round the
   land
On each I judge Thy foe."

—Alexander Pope

Forgive us, Lord Jesus, for the things we have done that make us feel uncomfortable in Thy presence. All the front that we polish so carefully for men to see, does not deceive Thee.

—Peter Marshall

"Help me, Father, to close my
  eyes,
To the faults that I would criticize;
Lord, teach me well the precious
  art,
Of looking for good in every
  heart."
                              —**Evans**

Of
Thanks

Praise be to thee
for our freedom
as men
not simply
to be thy children
but to choose to be.
　　　—**Fredrick Buechner**

I thank God for the bitter things;
They've been a "friend" to grace;
They've driven me from the paths
of ease
To storm the secret place.
—Florence White Willett

Thank you God for being at your
   best
When I am at my worst.
                —**Max Lucado** (para.)

Let all of us . . . Give thanks to God . . . to those eternal truths and universal principles of Holy Scripture which have inspired such measure of true greatness as this nation has achieved.

—Dwight D. Eisenhower

Let us . . . give thanks to God for his graciousness and generosity to us—pledge to him our everlasting devotion—beseech his divine guidance and the wisdom and strength to recognize and follow that guidance.

—Lyndon B. Johnson

O Lord, that lends me life,
Lend me a heart replete with
  thankfulness!
—**Shakespeare
  (King Henry the Sixth)**

Whatever my pleas and prayers and supplications, Lord, I am thankful just to be.

That out of the dark mystery of nonexistence, the priceless secret stuff of life was gathered to fashion me.

—Marjorie Holmes

In Times
of Loneliness

O Lord Jesus, help us to know that when we reach up to Thee, Thou art reaching down to us.

—Peter Marshall

Oh Thou who art at home
Deep in my heart
Enable me to join you
Deep in my heart.

—The Talmud

A weary Christian lay awake one night trying to hold the world together by his worrying. Then he heard the Lord gently say to him, "Now you go to sleep. I'll sit up."

—**Anon.**

Lord Jesus Christ, Help us not to fall in love with the night that covers us but through the darkness to watch for you as well as to work for you; to dream and hunger in the dark for the light of you.

—Fredrick Buechner

Teach me, my God and King
In all things Thee to see,
And what I do in anything,
To do it as for Thee.

—George Herbert

Aim at heaven and you will get
earth thrown in. Aim at earth and
you will get neither.

—C.S. Lewis

63

I came about like a well-handled
ship.
There stood at the wheel that . . .
steersman whom we call God.
—**Robert Louis Stevenson**

Be not far from me,
For trouble is near;
For there is none to help

—**Ps. 22:11**

Lord, many canoes will bump
  upon my shores today,
Give them a reason to want to
  stay.

—Anon.

66

In Times
of Loss

Truly terrible is the mystery of death.

I lament at the sight of the beauty created for us in the image of God which lies now in the grave . . . What is this mystery that surrounds us? . . . Why are we bound to death?

—John of Damascus

Surely He has borne our griefs
And carried our sorrows.

—Isa. 53:4a

Therefore my heart is glad, and
   my glory rejoices;
My flesh also will rest in hope.
You will show me the path of life;
In Your presence is fullness of joy;
At Your right hand are pleasures
   forevermore.

—Ps. 16:9,11

Be praised, my Lord,
for our sister, bodily death, from
whom no living thing can escape.
Blessed are those whom she finds
doing your most holy will, for the
second death cannot harm them.

—Francis of Assisi

Lord, you are the Alpha and the Omega. Behold, you make all things new.

—Anon.

Jesus, thank you for submerging yourself into the water of death so that we would know *Death Has Been Conquered!*

—**Max Lucado** (para.)

In my beginning is my end
In my end is my beginning
—**T.S. Eliot**

"The tears . . . streamed down, and I let them flow as freely as they would, making of them a pillow for my heart. On them it rested."

—Augustine

Almighty God, we remember your faithful servant; we pray that, having opened to him the gates of larger life, you will receive him more and more into your joyful service.

—Book of Common Prayer

For
Direction

"And now, Lord, what do I wait
   for?
My hope is in You."

—**Ps. 39:7**

"Teach us, Good Lord, to serve
thee as Thou deservest;
To give and not to count the
cost; . . .
To labor and not to ask for any
reward;
Save that of knowing that we do
Thy will."

—Ignatius

79

O GOD, You are my God;
Early will I seek You;
My soul thirsts for You;
My flesh longs for You
In a dry and thirsty land
Where there is no water.

—Ps. 63:1

80

Show me the way, Lord, let my
   light shine
As an example of good to
   mankind;
Help them to see the patterns of
   Thee,
Shining in beauty, lived out in me.

—Neuer

If God sees the sparrow fall,
Paints the lilies short and tall,
gives the skies their azure hue,
Will He not then care for you?

—Anon.

O Lord, help me to understand that You ain't goin' to let nuthin come my way that You and me together can't handle.

—Southern Prayer

A prayer to be said
When the world has gotten you
down,
and you feel rotten
and you're too doggone tired to
pray,
and you're in a big hurry,
and besides, you're mad at
everybody. . . . Help.

—**Charles Swindoll**

84

Be our light in the darkness, O Lord, and in Your great mercy defend us from all perils and dangers of this night; for the love of Your only Son, our Savior Jesus Christ. Amen.

—Book of Common Prayer

"When you are in the dark, listen, and God will give you a very precious message for someone else when you get into the light."

—Oswald Chambers

For
Hope

In my distress I called upon the
    LORD,
And cried out to my God;
He heard my voice from His
    temple,
And my cry came before Him,
even to His ears.

—Ps. 18:6

Why are you cast down, O my
soul?
And why are you disquieted
within me?
Hope in God, for I shall yet praise
Him
For the help of His countenance.

—**Ps. 42:5**

My voice You shall hear in the
   morning, O LORD;
In the morning I will direct it to
   You,
And I will look up.

—Ps. 5:3

"I know that You can do
   everything,
And that no purpose of Yours can
   be withheld from You."

—Job 42:2

Thank you God for brushing
The dark clouds from my mind
And leaving only sunshine
And joy of heart behind.

—**Unknown**

Sunk in this gray
depression
I cannot pray.
How can I give
expression
when ther're no words to say?

—Ruth Bell Graham

When in the midst of life with its
   problems,
Bent with our toil and burdens we
   bear,
Wonderful thought and deep
   consolation:
Jesus is always there!

—Lillenas

**Library of Congress
Cataloging-in-Publication Data**

Prayers.
    p.   cm.
    "A Janet Thoma book."
    ISBN 0-8407-7815-5
    1. Prayers.
BV260.P73   1993
242'.8—dc20   92–39094
                                            CIP

Printed in Singapore.
1 2 3 4 5 6 - 98 97 96 95 94 93